# LONDON COACH OPERATORS IN COLOUR: 1950-1980

Jef Johnson

IAN ALLAN Publishing

First published 1997

ISBN 0 7110 2496 0

© Jef Johnson 1997

Published by Ian Allan Publishing

an imprint of Ian Allan Ltd, Terminal House, Station Approach, Shepperton, Surrey TW17 8AS.

Printed by Ian Allan Printing Ltd, at its works at Coombelands in Runnymede, England.

Code: 9704/B3

*Front cover:*
Samuelson's, affectionately known as 'Sammy's', received four rare Duple (Northern) Dragonfly-bodied AEC Reliances in 1963. 450 FXX is departing from Victoria coach station in this March 1964 scene. The Dragonfly was designed at the former Burlingham factory in Blackpool and only six were ever built, the other two being Leyland Leopards operated by Fishwick's of Leyland. *David Warren*

*Previous page:*
Banfield's Coaches of Peckham acquired many operators over the years, the most famous being the Empire's Best fleet of Webber Brothers, Wood Green, taken over in July 1960. Empire's Best ran a regular daily service to Clacton via Chelmsford and Colchester, and Banfield's maintained the service using vehicles painted in Empire's Best livery. The Webber Brothers' fleet of AECs and Bedfords was sold after the takeover and replaced by a number of second-hand Leyland Tiger Cubs, including 289 BMV with a Duple Elizabethan body which was new to Venture, Hendon, in 1954. It is seen parked in Brighton in September 1964 while working a Banfield's excursion.
*David Warren*

# Introduction

London has always been home to a large number of coach operators, but the illustrations contained in this book represent only a small proportion of those in business during the period from the 1950s up to the end of the 1970s. Many colour transparencies of buses in London were taken by photographers during this time, but coaches were largely ignored. Fortunately, a few far-sighted individuals recorded the vehicles of London coach operators in colour, and hence it was possible to compile this book.

The area it covers is that of the former Metropolitan Traffic Area, which included Middlesex and parts of Kent, Surrey, Berkshire, Buckinghamshire, Bedfordshire, Hertfordshire and Essex.

The selection of illustrations was limited by the small amount of material available. However, I have managed to feature most of the major coach operators, together with a few of the smaller companies. Many of the operators are no longer in business and I hope that the photographs evoke fond memories. Names that spring to mind are Banfield's, Birch Bros, Cronshaw's, Glenton Tours, Samuelson's, Surrey Motors, Timpson's, Valliant and Venture. Among those that have survived are Banstead Coaches, Crawley Luxury, Epsom Coaches, Frames Rickards, Grey-Green, Harris of Grays, Limebourne, Mitcham Belle and Safeguard. Most of the operators have long and sometimes complicated histories, and unravelling these was a time-consuming yet enjoyable task. It was interesting to trace the development of a company from its humble origins through to becoming a major operator.

The early 1950s saw the introduction of underfloor-engined vehicles which immediately made half-cab coaches seem very old-fashioned. London operators were quick to introduce such vehicles into their fleets, although front-engined vehicles, such as the Bedford SB and Ford Thames Trader, remained popular for lighter duties. By the 1960s most half-cab types had been withdrawn. No suitable illustrations of such vehicles came to light during my research and therefore these are not illustrated. The expansion of the motorway network in the 1960s led to a demand for larger and more powerful vehicles.

Since 1950, the maximum legal length of a single-deck coach had been 30ft (approximately 9m). In 1961 this was increased to 36ft (11m) and in 1968 it was increased again to 39ft 4in (12m).

It is not only operators that have faded into history. All of the British chassis manufacturers except one (Dennis) featured in the pages of this book have disappeared too. AEC, Bedford, Bristol, Commer, Ford and Leyland are now just a memory. Continental manufacturers such as Volvo and DAF entered the British market during the 1970s, offering very competitive designs. These companies gradually gained a strong foothold in the market which, together with other problems, forced the British manufacturers out of business. It is a similar story with coachbuilders.

Many operators offered services to coastal resorts and most of them thrived on this type of business. Coastal work started to decline during the 1970s, but at the same time there was an increase in sightseeing and touring work for incoming tourists. This was a result of air travel becoming more popular because of cheaper fares, more frequent services and faster and larger aircraft. The development of London's three major airports, Heathrow, Gatwick and Stansted, resulted in a heavy influx of tourists into the capital.

I would like to thank the photographers, without whom the book could not have been produced. Special thanks are due to Terry Torch, who checked the captions and added many useful facts about the operators. A number of publications were consulted in my research, in particular those produced by the PSV Circle. The two British Bus Fleet booklets covering London coach operators, published by Ian Allan in 1963 and 1967, proved to be a valuable source of information. Thank you also to my wife, Wendy, for putting up with my spending many long hours ensconced in my study.

*Jef Johnson*
*Isleworth*
*October 1996*

*Right:*
In 1963 Banfield's purchased three new Bedford VAL14/Duple Vega Majors, CMD 204A in standard two-tone green livery and CMD 205/6A in Empire's Best livery. One of the latter is pictured here when only two months old, together with CMD 204A, in Morden Road, Merton, in September 1963.
*Geoffrey Morant collection*

*Right:*
The traditional two-tone green livery of Banfield's was changed to this mustard and white scheme during the early 1970s. MHX 914C was a Leyland Leopard PSU3/3 with a Duple (Northern) Continental body, one of two bought new in 1965, and is seen in Culverden Road, Balham, in December 1972. Banfield's were taken over by Gold Case Travel of Middlesbrough in 1974 and were renamed Bee-Line Roadways in 1975. Gold Case Travel closed the operation in 1979.
*Mike Barbour*

3

Banstead Coaches commenced operations in 1950 with a Bedford OB and continued to buy further Bedfords including HJM 5, a petrol-engined Bedford SB3/Plaxton Embassy. It was new to Silver Badge Motors of Windermere in March 1961 and was purchased by Banstead Coaches exactly one year later. It is seen at Whitehawk coach park, Brighton, in October 1965.
*David Warren*

Bexleyheath Transport was established by a member of the Margo family
before World War 1 and was another enthusiastic operator of Bedfords. FYW
807J was one of a batch of seven YRQs with Plaxton Panorama Elite II bodies
purchased in 1971 and this photograph shows the vehicle at Gloucester Green
bus station in Oxford. The company closed down in April 1988.
*Peter Tulloch collection*

Birch Bros were one of the pioneer motorbus operators in London in the early part of this century and continued to operate in the capital until 1934 when the services and vehicles were compulsorily taken over by London Transport. The coach side of the business continued with private hire and excursions and a London to Rushden service which was introduced in 1928. Local stage services were also operated in the Bedford and Hitchin areas. RYT 31 was one of six AEC Reliance/Weymann Fanfares supplied in 1956 and is seen in Pancras Road, King's Cross, the departure point for the Rushden service, in 1963. *Vic Nutton, courtesy Geoff Lumb collection*

In 1960/61 five AEC Reliances with unusual Willowbrook Viscount bodies were added to the fleet. These featured a 'Ford Anglia'-style backward-sloping rear window; the only other bodies of this design were supplied to the Grey Cars fleet of Devon General. 46 AUW is pictured picking up at Bedford bus station in July 1967. *Geoff Lumb*

The first Leyland Leopards in the Birch fleet were two of the L2 variety with
Duple Britannia bodies supplied in 1961. 80 CYV is standing in Eversholt
Street, Euston, sandwiched between two Ford Zephyr Mark IIs while working a
private hire journey.
*Peter Tulloch collection*

Further AEC Reliances were purchased in 1964, this time a batch of five with Harrington Grenadier bodies. These were to be Birch's last AECs and their first and only Harrington bodies. ALD 28B is seen at Brighton's Whitehawk coach park in October 1965. *David Warren*

In 1968 Birch Bros abandoned their stage routes in Bedfordshire and the following year sold their London to Rushden routes together with 12 vehicles to United Counties. The private hire and excursions business continued until 1971 when this was purchased by the Ewer Group, who took over nine vehicles including this 1969 Bedford VAM70/Plaxton Panorama Elite. VLF 35G is depicted at Wembley in May 1970 in the final style of Birch livery. *Alec Swain*

10

Following trials in 1965 with a Standerwick Leyland Atlantean coach, BOAC ordered 15 similar vehicles with Metro-Cammell bodies for their service from Central London to Heathrow Airport. They were delivered in the following year and had 54 seats and rear luggage compartments. LYF 317D is departing from the Airways Terminal in Buckingham Palace Road, Victoria. *Chris Aston*

11

Belgian coachbuilder Van Hool entered the British coach market in 1969 and in 1973 joined forces with McArdle of Dundalk to take over the bus building activities of CIE, the Irish national transport operator. In addition to building buses for CIE, the new company, known as Van Hool-McArdle, produced coaches for the British market to Van Hool's established 300 design. A number were supplied to London operators including Cavalier Coaches of Hounslow who received eight in 1977 on Bedford YMT chassis. Photographed outside the Hilton Hotel (now called the Moat House) in Stratford-upon-Avon on a dull June day in 1978, SUR 289R is operating under contract to Travellers International. *Chris Shaw*

City Coach Lines was established in 1968 as a subsidiary of Passenger Vehicle Sales, Upminster, and was associated with Super Coaches of Upminster, both companies purchasing a number of new Leyland Leopard coaches in the late 1960s and early 1970s. AYU 201H was a PSU3A/4R type with a Plaxton Panorama Elite body and is seen at City's Upminster depot when brand-new in May 1970.
*Mike Barbour*

13

*Above:*
City also added second-hand Leopards to their fleet, including this Harrington Cavalier-bodied example, PCK 619, acquired in early 1970 from Ribble. It was new to Ribble in 1961 and had been used by them on extended tours, having only 32 well-spaced seats. City entered it in the 1970 Brighton Coach Rally and this picture shows it parked on Madeira Drive while taking part in that event.
*David Warren*

*Right:*
Clubb's of Wilmington, near Dartford, added three new Bedford VAL14/Duple Vega Majors to their small fleet in 1965, including JNK 248C which was entered in the following year's Brighton Coach Rally. It is seen here cruising along Madeira Drive, watched with interest by two young enthusiasts. Note the BBC van in the background, which was there to cover the event for television and radio. Clubb's ceased operating coaches at the end of 1974.
*David Warren*

*Left:*
Continental Pioneer of Richmond was founded in 1964 to specialise in the operation of camping tours to Europe. In May 1968 former London Transport route 235 (Richmond Town Centre to Richmond Hill) was taken over from Isleworth Coaches who had operated the route since January 1966. The fleet consisted mainly of second-hand vehicles, but one of those bought new was VHV 83S, one of two Leyland Leopard PSU3E/4Rs with Plaxton Viewmaster Express bodies. It was only two months old when photographed at their depot in Cedar Terrace, Richmond, in March 1978. Continental Pioneer ceased trading in 1986.
*Mike Barbour*

The last vehicles purchased by Conway Hunt of Ottershaw, Surrey, were four
Bedford YRTs with Duple Dominant bodies. The first of the batch, UPH 203M,
is pictured at Hastings coach park in November 1974. It continued in service
until the business ceased trading in 1985. Conway Hunt also controlled
Kingston Luxury Coaches and Starway Coaches of Surbiton, all three fleets
using the same grey and primrose livery. *Mike Barbour*

The Luton-based Court Line empire included a travel agency, an airline and a coach company. The latter resulted from the takeover of Hillside Coaches of Luton in 1971, and stage services in the Luton and Dunstable areas were started in the following year. In August 1974 the group spectacularly collapsed although the coach business continued until December 1974, the stage services being taken over by United Counties. YXD 472M was a Ford R1114/Duple Dominant, photographed outside St Paul's Cathedral on 17 August 1974, the day after the announcement of the collapse of the company. *Mike Barbour*

Duple's Viceroy design was introduced at the 1966 Commercial Motor Show and continued in production until late 1972 when it was superseded by the Dominant. A late example of the Viceroy was Crawley Luxury Coaches' SPX 63K, bought new in May 1972 and mounted on a Ford R226 chassis. It is seen at the company's garage in November 1973. *Mike Barbour*

An interesting line-up of vehicles owned by Cresta Coaches of Wimbledon, photographed at their Toynbee Road yard, near Wimbledon Chase station, in October 1968. BAX 900B was an unusual Karrier D98A with Reading 14-seat coachwork, new to Henley's of Abertillery, Monmouthshire, in 1964 and purchased by Cresta in 1968. UDB 101/2 were petrol-engined Bedford SB3s with Duple Super Vega bodies which arrived in 1967 from Altrincham Coachways, a subsidiary of North Western, having been part of a batch of eight vehicles new in 1961. *Mike Barbour*

In 1913 Mr Lewis Cronshaw purchased a garage business in Blackburn, Lancashire, and in 1916 started operating coach excursions. Some years later he met the sub-postmistress from Hendon who persuaded him to base some of his coaches in the northwest London suburb. The Hendon branch of the business continued to grow and in 1960 the Blackburn garage closed and the rival business of Venture of Hendon was purchased. In 1966 both Cronshaw and Venture became part of the Earls Court Holdings Group who had taken over Valliant Direct Coaches of Ealing in the previous year, the combined company becoming Valliant-Cronshaw. The Cronshaw fleet of the early 1960s comprised Bedfords, Fords and Leylands, all bodied at the nearby Duple works. 4556 MD was a Bedford SB5 with Duple Super Vega coachwork, one of two new in 1962. It is seen in May 1963 on an excursion to Corfe Castle in Dorset. *Cyril Cowland*

Epsom Coaches was established in 1920 by the partnership of Messrs Richmond and Reeves. In 1933 the company became H. R. Richmond Ltd and continued trading as Epsom Coaches, except for a period in the mid-1960s when the H. R. Richmond Ltd fleetname was used. MPA 552D, a Bedford VAM14/Duple Bella Venture, was one of the vehicles which carried this fleetname and is pictured taking part in the 1966 Brighton Coach Rally. *David Warren*

Between 1975 and 1982, 12 Bristol LHS midi-coaches with Plaxton Supreme bodies were purchased. One of the first batch of three, GNM 232N, was involved in an unfortunate accident in 1976 which resulted in extensive damage to the vehicle. The chassis was rebuilt and received a new Plaxton Supreme body together with a new registration number, UGC 229R. It is seen here waiting to depart from the company's Blenheim Road garage.
*Epsom Coaches collection*

23

The main business of Essex County Coaches, based in the Stratford area of East London, was the operation of tours on behalf of the Workers Travel Association (WTA) with whom the company had close connections. Galleon World Travel, successors to the WTA, became the owners of the company and the Galleon Tours fleetname was adopted. Like Glenton Tours, Essex County continued to specify centre entrances long after front entrances had become standard on underfloor-engined coaches. AJD 528C was one of five AEC Reliances with Plaxton Panorama bodies delivered in 1965 which had this feature and is seen in Minster Street, Salisbury, while on a Galleon tour in April 1968.
*David Warren*

The fleet became standardised on the AEC Reliance/Plaxton combination until
production of the Reliance ceased in 1979. The 1965 Reliances were the last
ones with centre entrances, all subsequent deliveries having front entrances. In
August 1975, KLK 452K — with Panorama Elite II bodywork — was captured
on tour in Oban carrying the livery introduced in 1967 to replace the
traditional maroon and cream colours. The company changed its name to
Galleon Tours Ltd in 1981 and ceased trading at the end of 1987.
*Cyril Cowland*

Evan Evans Tours is one of the best known names in the incoming tourist sightseeing market. Mr Evan Evans set up The Woburn Garage (London) Ltd in 1929 and traded as Evans Transport Enterprises, the sightseeing tours becoming a major part of the business. In 1969 The Woburn Garage group was purchased by Wallace Arnold who continued the Evan Evans operation until 1983 when it changed hands again, passing to Insight International. A number of small vehicles were operated in the 1960s including 8158 AP, a 1964 Bedford J2SZ2 goods chassis fitted with Duple (Midland) Compact bodywork. In August 1968 it was waiting at Windsor station for the return of its passengers who were probably visiting Windsor Castle at the time.
*Mike Barbour*

Bedfords bodied by either Thurgood or Duple had been the mainstay of the fleet until 1966 when the Ford R-series became the standard vehicle. KPM 383E was an example of the longer R226 with Plaxton Panorama bodywork delivered in 1967 and is seen parked outside the company's depot in Purchese Street, St Pancras, on a gloomy April day in the following year. It was retained in the fleet under Wallace Arnold ownership until 1972. *Mike Barbour*

In 1967 Evan Evans decided to enter the executive coach market with this luxurious vehicle, LAP 665E, named Black Knight. It had 27 reclining seats, tables and a bar but unfortunately it was built on the unreliable Daimler Roadliner chassis with a rear-mounted Cummins V6 engine. A second Roadliner with similarly equipped Duple Commander III body, Quicksilver, was purchased in 1968 and five further Roadliners were ordered for 1969, but these were cancelled by Wallace Arnold. Both vehicles were retained by Wallace Arnold until 1972 and LAP 665E was even fitted with a Perkins V8 engine in 1970 which did little to improve its reliability. When new it was entered in the 1967 Brighton Coach Rally where it was runner-up in the Concours d'Elégance. *David Warren*

Four Bedford VAS/Duples were added to the fleet between 1962 and 1967, the final one being LPM 983E with Duple's Vista 25 style of body. It turned out to be the last Bedford purchased by the company and was photographed at Brighton in July 1969, a few months after the Wallace Arnold takeover.
*David Warren*

Fountain Luxury Coaches of Twickenham was established in the 1930s. Their coaches were often named after contemporary airliners and GMF 256B, pictured here at Brighton's Whitehawk coach park in November 1964, was Elizabethan, other examples being Comet, Viscount, Ambassador and Britannia (aptly carried by a Duple Britannia-bodied AEC Reliance). GMF 256B was one of four Bedford SB5s delivered in May 1964 with Plaxton Embassy bodies. The company came under the control of the Blackford family, proprietors of Isleworth Coaches, in 1974. *David Warren*

Frames Tours of Bloomsbury can trace its roots back to 1881 when John Frame Senior, a tailor from Preston, started organising railway excursions. Three years later, sightseeing tours of London were introduced using horse-drawn brakes, with motor vehicles taking over during the early 1920s. After World War 2 Bedford OBs and SBs were purchased, followed in 1955 by an AEC Reliance which quickly became the standard choice for heavyweight vehicles until 1969 when two Leyland Leopards arrived. 7946 ML was a 1962 example with Plaxton Embassy I bodywork, captured basking in the sun at Hants & Dorset's Winchester garage in August 1964. *David Warren*

31

In 1972 five AEC Reliance/Plaxton Panorama Elite IIs with unusual dual entrances arrived. The second entrance was designed to speed up boarding and alighting time. CAR 164/5K and CAR 167/8K were in Frames livery, while CAR 166K was in the maroon and black livery of Rickards of Brentford, a subsidiary of Frames since 1967. CAR 164K is seen in April 1974 at Bodiam Castle, Sussex, awaiting the return of some of its passengers (and its driver!). *Cyril Cowland*

Glenton Tours was started in the early 1920s by two coach drivers, one of whom lived in Glenton Road, Lewisham. In 1928 they encountered financial difficulties and sold the company to the Saxton family who were in the estate agency business. The Saxtons steadily expanded the company, specialising in quality tours using vehicles offering the highest degree of comfort. In 1932 the first of many Dennis coaches arrived and that make was purchased almost exclusively until 1961, by which time the AEC Reliance was beginning to find favour. Ten underfloor-engined Lancet UFs entered the fleet between 1954 and 1961, UYW 69 being a 1958 example with Plaxton Consort bodywork. It is parked in Penzance while on a West Country tour in this September 1964 view. *Cyril Cowland*

The AEC Reliance/Plaxton combination became the standard choice in the 1960s and centre entrances continued to be specified on most of its coaches until 1981. BAN 116H was one of four 10m examples purchased in 1970 with Panorama Elite bodies which had only 34 seats, indicating the level of comfort offered. In May 1972 it was on tour in the Lake District and is seen taking a break in the coach park at Keswick. *Mike Barbour*

34

In 1974 the company purchased its first Volvos, although a final batch of AECs entered service in 1976, followed by two Leyland Leopards in 1977. Thereafter all new additions to the fleet were of Volvo manufacture with either Plaxton or Duple bodies. VUL 160S was one of five B58s, new in 1978, with Plaxton Supreme 38-seat bodies. It is seen here when brand-new in April 1978 at Gloucester Green bus station, Oxford. At the end of 1988 Glenton Tours decided to cease operating its own coaches and contract out the operation of its tours to Tellings-Golden Miller of Weybridge. The six newest Glenton vehicles passed to Tellings-Golden Miller who also painted eight of their own coaches in Glenton livery. *Geoffrey Morant*

The origins of Golden Miller go back to 1923 when Mr F. G. Wilder started a haulage business in the Feltham area. In 1955 the company diversified into coach operation with a Bedford OB and later the same year the Golden Miller business of Fred Varney was taken over. In 1967 Tourist Coachways of Hounslow's stage service from Feltham station to East Bedfont was acquired and over the following years a number of local stage services were developed.

However, coaching remained the most important part of the business. The pride of the fleet in 1966 was this Ford R192/Duple Viscount which featured air-conditioning, an unusual feature in those days. LLK 762D is seen at that year's Brighton Coach Rally where it scooped the award for the highest-placed Ford in the road section.

*David Warren*

Beach's of Staines was acquired by Golden Miller in 1977 and their name is carried on the front of APH 521T, a Bedford YMT/Plaxton Supreme IV new in 1979. In this February 1980 scene at the company's depot in Fern Grove, Feltham, it is receiving its daily washdown. Control of Golden Miller passed to Telling's of Weybridge in 1985 and two years later the two fleets were merged to form Tellings-Golden Miller. *Geoffrey Morant*

George Ewer established a handcart business in the Shoreditch area of London in 1885. Horse-drawn carts were added in the early 1900s and in 1919 the first motor vehicle was purchased. The Grey-Green Coaches fleetname was adopted and the company flourished to become one of the most well-known names in the coach industry. Harrington's of Hove had been patronised for coachwork since the early 1930s and became the major supplier in the postwar period. The Cavalier was their most successful design and many examples entered the Grey-Green fleet, including 428 EYY on a Leyland Leopard L2 chassis which was new in January 1963. It is seen on the edge of a sea of coaches at Wembley Stadium coach park while on hire to Dix Luxury Coaches of Dagenham in April 1970. The Dix business was itself taken over by the Ewer Group in 1976.
*Alec Swain*

*Right:*

The Grenadier design was a restyled version of the Cavalier introduced in 1962, although the Cavalier remained available until Harrington ceased coachbuilding in 1966. One of the first Grenadiers was Grey-Green's 427 EYY which was displayed on the Harrington stand at the 1962 Commercial Motor Show held at Earls Court, entering service in January 1963. It was based on a Leyland Leopard PSU3/3RT chassis and carried an experimental livery with more cream and no grey, but this was not perpetuated. In June 1963 it was at Colchester bus station awaiting departure to London on one of Grey-Green's many express services serving East Anglia. *David Warren*

*Right:*

Four Leyland Leopard L2Ts with Grenadier bodies entered service in December 1964 and introduced a revised livery featuring more cream. Three of them, CLK 474/2/1B, are lined up at Jubilee Gardens on the South Bank, near Waterloo station, in this October 1966 view while on a private hire duty.
*Mike Barbour*

39

Duple were the other main supplier of coachwork to the Ewer Group, mostly on lightweight chassis. JUV 514D was one of 39 Leyland-engined Bedford VAM14s with Duple Bella Venture bodies delivered in 1966 and is seen at Grey-Green's Stamford Hill garage in November 1967, parked next to the company's BMC Minivan publicity vehicle. *Mike Barbour*

The Grey-Green livery was revised again in 1971 to this simplified scheme of white and green. The two other subsidiaries at the time, Birch Bros and Orange Luxury, adopted a similar style but with the green replaced by red and orange respectively. The Ewer Group switched allegiance to Plaxton in 1969, although ONK 642H, pictured here at Victoria coach station in October 1975 working on hire to National Express, was transferred from World Wide Coaches of Camberwell in April 1974 when that concern was acquired. It was a Leyland Leopard PSU3A/4R with Plaxton Panorama Elite body and was new to World Wide in 1970.
*Mike Barbour*

41

The MCW group started building coach bodies in 1954 when the Fanfare design, produced at the Weymann factory in Addlestone, Surrey, was introduced for mounting on AEC, Guy and Leyland chassis. Together with its Castilian and Beacon derivatives, it was sold mainly to BET companies. In 1962 an unsuccessful attempt was made to break into the independent sector with the Amethyst and Topaz designs for Bedford SB and VAL chassis respectively. At the 1966 Commercial Motor Show the Athena design was launched, but, before production got under way, it was restyled as the Metropolitan. 34 Metropolitans were built on Bedford VAM chassis between 1967 and 1969 and many of them were sold to London operators. Ten further Metropolitans were built in 1969 under licence by Strachans of Hamble on Ford R192 chassis. Grove Coaches of West Norwood purchased NAA 308F, a Bedford VAM5 example, in 1968 and it is seen here in November 1970 parked in Balham High Road. *Mike Barbour*

Frank Harris's family had been involved in horse-drawn road haulage since the late 19th century. In 1923 Mr Harris set up a coach business and from 1927 a number of workmen's and dockworkers' services were operated in the Grays and Purfleet areas. These services were acquired by London Transport in 1934 leaving Mr Harris to concentrate on coaching and road haulage. In 1958 two limited companies were created: Frank Harris (Coaches) Ltd for the coach activities and Harris Haulage (Grays) Ltd for the lorries. AEC, Bedford and Leyland were the favoured chassis types with coachwork by Duple, Harrington or Yeates. The AEC/Duple combination is represented here by 284 NVX, a 1959 Reliance with the Britannia style of body, at Victoria coach station in July 1968 while operating on hire to Maidstone & District. Parked next to it is HPN 482D, a 1966 Ford R192/Duple Empress of Cliff's Saloon Coaches of Eltham. *Mike Barbour*

The Harris fleet contained a number of Bedfords with Harrington bodies. The last three purchased were VAL14s with what was to be Harrington's final design, the Legionnaire. LVX 320C, the last of the three, was actually a Legionnaire II which had a shallower roof than the original design. This view shows it on Epsom Downs in June 1969, bringing punters to the Derby.

Harrington were planning to develop this design for underfloor-engined chassis when, at the end of 1965, they decided to cease coachbuilding. It was intended to unveil the new design at the 1966 Commercial Motor Show. *Mike Barbour*

Knightswood Coaches of Watford was established in 1949 by the partnership of Messrs Withey and Berney. In the following year Mr Berney was replaced by Mr Druce and a limited company was formed in 1951. A stage service between Watford and Elstree Aerodrome was started in 1964. Operations continued until 1975, when a new company, Campbell Consultants Ltd, was formed to take over Knightswood and fellow Watford operator H. & C. Transport. HRO 331G was a Bedford VAS5/Plaxton Panorama I new in 1969 and is seen passing through its home town in September 1976. Campbell Consultants ceased trading in 1984.

*Geoffrey Morant*

Lewis of Farnborough (Kent) received a batch of 12 brand-new coaches in 1962, 101-112 DLL, all Ford Thames Trader 510Es with unusual Burlingham Gannet bodies. 105 DLL is pictured at Whitehawk coach park, Brighton, in July 1964, two years before the company was taken over by Timpson's. The Gannet, introduced at the end of 1961, was a development of the Seagull 60 and 61 designs, and was the last design to carry the Burlingham name, the company having been taken over by Duple in 1960. At the end of 1962 the Gannet was restyled to become the Duple (Northern) Firefly. *David Warren*

Limebourne Coaches was established in 1970 by Mr Paul Campana and Mr Peter Inzani, originally operating from a base in Putney. In 1973 the company moved to its present depot in Silverthorne Road, Battersea, and in the same year eight Bedford YRTs with Plaxton Panorama Elite III bodies were delivered.

Two of them, LJH 243/6L, were photographed in March 1973, a few days after entering service, in Palace Street, Victoria. LJH 243L carries the fleetname of Saintseal Travel, Limebourne's main customer at the time. Limebourne became part of Q Drive in 1995. *Mike Barbour*

Limebourne acquired control of R&S Travel, Kensington, in August 1976 and operated it as a subsidiary until June 1978. JYM 743N was one of two Bedford YRTs purchased by R&S in 1975 which had the first production examples of Willowbrook's Spacecar body. It was transferred to the parent fleet in May 1976 and is seen shortly afterwards at St Pancras Station, having been repainted in SAGA Holidays livery with Woodbourne fleetnames. Woodbourne was a short-lived subsidiary of Limebourne Coaches. *Mike Barbour*

One of the first DAFs to enter service in this country was TGK 192R of Mitcham Belle Coaches. It had a Van Hool 300 series body and was exhibited at the 1976 Commercial Motor Show, entering service in the following April. It is seen in June 1978 on Epsom Downs while attending The Derby. Mitcham Belle Coaches was started in the 1920s by Mr W. Blunt and continued operating until 1967 when control of the business, together with its Robin & Rambler subsidiary, passed to Mr Fred Wilde who traded as Wimbledon Coaches. Mr Wilde subsequently adopted the Mitcham Belle fleetname. *Mike Barbour*

National Travel (South East) came into being on 1 January 1974 and was an amalgamation of the National Bus Company's three London-based coach concerns: Tillings Transport, Timpson's and Samuelson's New Transport. The standard National white livery was adopted, and early purchases were three Bedford YRTs with Willowbrook's newly introduced Spacecar body, new in 1975. JMY 123N was parked outside the entrance to Samuelson's garage in Eccleston Place, Victoria, in this August 1975 view. *Mike Barbour*

Orange Luxury Coaches was an old established company based in Brixton and had been owned by the Keith & Boyle organisation until 1953, when it was acquired by the Ewer Group. The company had the distinction of holding a Royal Warrant for passenger transport of the Royal Household. Ewer's operated Orange Luxury as a separate subsidiary until 1975, although a few coaches continued to carry the Orange fleetname and Royal Warrant insignia until 1979, the year in which the Warrant lapsed. The 50 vehicles taken over in 1953 were Bedford OBs and SBs with Duple bodies, mostly petrol-engined, but these were gradually replaced by new diesel-engined Bedfords painted in an 'orange' version of Grey-Green livery. Four Bristol LH6L/Plaxton Panorama Elite IIs were purchased in 1972, three allocated to Orange and one to the newly acquired Birch subsidiary. JRK 626K is seen in November of that year passing along Pall Mall, Piccadilly, operating on hire to Thomas Cook & Sons. *Geoffrey Morant*

AEC Reliance/Plaxton Panorama Elite II GBU 201K had three owners within the space of two years. It was new to Phipps Blue Riband Tours of Bloomsbury in April 1972 and two months later it became part of the World Wide Coaches fleet when that company acquired the Phipps business. After the Ewer Group gained control of World Wide in April 1974 it was transferred to the Orange fleet. It was photographed on a sunny March day in 1976. *Geoffrey Morant*

The smallest company within the BET group was Red Line Continental Motorways who operated only a handful of vehicles. It was a direct descendant of the Red Line Omnibus Company, the once famous London independent bus operator based in Portobello Road, North Kensington, and developed its coaching activities after the bus routes were taken over by London Transport in 1933. The BET group acquired the company, together with Blue Cars Continental Coach Cruises, in 1953. The two companies were eventually merged, trading as Red Line and operating from Red Line's original garage in Portobello Road. TLN 4 was an AEC Reliance with Harrington Wayfarer IV body, new in 1957 and photographed in Arundel Street, Brighton, in September 1966. *David Warren*

The last vehicle purchased by Red Line was this 1963 AEC Reliance with Duple (Northern) Continental body, acquired from fellow London operator Global Tours in 1967. The company was wound up the following year, prior to the formation of the National Bus Company. 280 HLC is pictured here in April 1967 while attending the 13th British Coach Rally, although not actually entered in the event. *David Warren*

The origins of Rickards go back to 1850, when Charles Rickard established a horse-cab business in Paddington. By 1912 motor charabancs were in use on sightseeing, private hire and touring work and the coach side of the business was gradually expanded. In 1936 the company was awarded a Royal Warrant for the hire of coaches to the Royal Household for special events. A fleet of limousines was also operated, together with several bullion vans on contract to the Great Western Railway. After World War 2 the company concentrated on its coaching activities and acquired Universal Sightseeing Tours in 1946. With the growth in air travel in the 1950s and 1960s, airport transfer work became an important part of the business. Rickards became a subsidiary of British Eagle International Airlines and in 1963 started the first Rail-Air Link service between Heathrow and High Wycombe. The headquarters moved from Paddington to Brentford in 1965 and, two years later, ownership of the company passed to Frames Tours. MRO 185L, a Bedford YRT with Plaxton Panorama Elite III body, displays the Royal Coat of Arms at Inverness while on tour in August 1976. *R L Wilson*

Arthur Newman, a coal and general haulier based in Guildford, fitted a charabanc body to one of his Daimler lorries in 1924. Further charabancs were added to the fleet and a number of coastal and racecourse excursions were developed. By 1926 the Safeguard Coaches name had been adopted and in the following year local bus services were started in competition with Aldershot & District. The business became a limited company in 1933. For many years locally-built Dennis buses and coaches were purchased, but after 1948 the company switched allegiance to AEC for buses and Bedford for coaches. 1920 PJ was a Bedford SB5 added to the fleet in 1963 with Duple's newly introduced Bella Vega body and is seen parked at Brighton in August 1964. *David Warren*

In 1920 Mr G. B. Samuelson, a film producer, started operating coaches to various coastal resorts, trading as Samuelson Saloon Coaches. The company was acquired by the Red & White group in 1931, but five years later was sold to London Coastal Coaches Ltd, the owners of Victoria coach station, who renamed it Samuelson New Transport Company Ltd. Early vehicles were of Dennis, ADC and Gilford manufacture, followed by a number of AEC Regals.

The first postwar vehicles were Leyland Royal Tigers with Duple Ambassador bodies, purchased in 1951, and were followed in 1953 by Duple-bodied AEC Reliances which became the standard choice until 1965. 442 BXD was a 1961 example with the Britannia style of body and was captured in August 1964 at Victoria coach station, sandwiched between Thames Valley and East Kent vehicles. *David Warren*

Leyland Leopards were purchased from 1965 onwards. The first batch of four had Harrington Grenadier bodies, as illustrated by DYM 454C parked inside Samuelson's garage at Eccleston Place, opposite Victoria coach station, in October 1966. Subsequent Leopards were bodied by either Duple (Northern) or Plaxton. The company operated a number of contracts for British United Airways, painting certain vehicles in their dark blue, white and silver livery. In the mid-1960s this was adopted as the standard fleet livery, replacing the traditional green and cream. *Mike Barbour*

Silverline was the trading name used by Hall's Coaches of Hounslow who concentrated on contract work for a number of major airlines, including Pan Am and TWA. VYH 55G was one of eight AEC Reliances with Plaxton Panorama Elite bodies added to the fleet in 1969 for this purpose and is seen here in September of that year carrying Pan Am livery at Heathrow Airport. Hall's took control of Valliant-Cronshaw in 1969 and certain vehicles received Valliant-Silverline fleetnames. In 1971 part of the Valliant-Cronshaw operation was sold off to a reactivated Venture Transport company based in Harrow (the original Venture Transport had been a subsidiary of Cronshaw's since 1960) and two years later Hall's itself was taken over by the Dunstable-based Tricentrol group, who set up a new company, Silverline Coaches Ltd, to continue operations. This lasted only until 1975, when Silverline ceased trading. *Geoffrey Morant*

Mr Ben Stanley of Hersham, Surrey, set up in business as a bus operator in the 1920s. He developed two routes, Hersham to Walton-on-Thames and Hersham to Weybridge, which were compulsorily taken over by London Transport in 1934. Mr Stanley retained his premises and concentrated on the coach side of the business which he built up to good effect. The company expanded in 1956 by taking over Bland's Coaches of Ripley and again in 1968 with the acquisition of the old-established Green Luxury Coaches of Walton-on-Thames. The wheel turned full circle in January 1978, when the Hersham Green to Walton-on-

Thames section of route 264 was taken over from London Transport, this being virtually the same as one of the routes surrendered in 1934 to London Transport. Early vehicles included Bedfords, Brockways, Fords and Maudslays, with Bedford and Foden becoming the popular choices in the postwar period. NAR 410M, a 1973 Bedford VAS5 with Plaxton Panorama body, is pictured in May 1976 at St Mark's Hill, Surbiton. Ben Stanley ceased trading in August 1985. *Cyril Cowland*

Super Coaches of Upminster was established in 1939, becoming a limited company in 1950. The stage services of Sterling Bus Service, Romford, were acquired in 1958 and, following the protracted London Transport strike in the same year, the company applied for a number of stage licences. These were granted and operated under the Upminster and District fleetname. In 1969 the business was taken over by Passenger Vehicle Sales, a local dealer with whom a close working relationship existed. The Super Coaches and Upminster and District operations passed to the associated business of City Coach Lines (Upminster) Ltd. The City business was split into two during 1971, the other part becoming Blue Line. City ceased trading early in 1973, while Blue Line lasted until October 1975. The Super fleet consisted mainly of Bedfords and Fords during the 1960s, a typical example being CMJ 209D, a Ford R192/Duple Viscount pictured at Brighton in June 1966. *David Warren*

Surrey Motors of Sutton will long be remembered for their immaculately turned out fleet of Harrington-bodied coaches. The company was started in 1919 by Mr William Rees Jeffreys and the association with Harrington was begun in 1933, when two AEC Regals were delivered. From then on virtually all new deliveries were bodied by Harrington, the very last one being HLP 11C which was one of three AEC Reliances with the Grenadier bodystyle received in 1965. Following Harrington's decision to cease bodybuilding at the end of 1965, the company turned to Plaxton. Sadly, Surrey Motors itself decided to cease operations at the end of April 1980, its licences being taken over by neighbouring operator Epsom Coaches. HLP 11C was photographed at Brighton's Whitehawk coach park in May 1967. *David Warren*

Tillings Transport was a direct descendant of Thomas Tilling Ltd, one of the earliest operators of motorbuses in London. The coach side of the company was developed after World War 1 and in 1925 the touring business of Pickfords was taken over. The Tilling organisation was nationalised in 1948, and a new company was formed under the name of Tillings Transport (BTC) Ltd to continue the coach operation in London. In 1951 the business of Pat Hearn, King's Cross, was acquired together with a fleet of 38 coaches. Prior to nationalisation, Tillings Transport had shown a preference for AEC chassis and this make continued to be purchased until 1952, albeit with ECW bodies, when a batch of five Regal IVs, identical to London Transport's RFW class, was delivered. From then on, the company came into line with its fellow nationalised operators by purchasing Bristol/ECW coaches. 2 BXB was a 1961 Bristol MW6G and is seen in 1963 at Grantown-on-Spey in the Scottish Highlands, in company with 13 DLY which had ECW's later style of MW body.
*Vic Nutton, courtesy Geoff Lumb collection*

13 DLY is seen again in this view taken at Melrose in July 1962 while on contract to Thomas Cook & Sons, one of Tilling's long-standing customers. During 1962 administrative control of the company passed to Eastern National, which resulted in subsequent new vehicles being registered in Essex instead of London. This vehicle was, in fact, the last one to receive a London registration mark. A couple of years later the distinctive Tilling livery of pearl grey and maroon was phased out in favour of Eastern National's cream and green. The company was renamed Tillings Transport (NBC) Ltd in 1969 upon formation of the National Bus Company, and in 1974 became part of National Travel (South East) along with Samuelson's and Timpson's. *Cyril Cowland*

Alexander Timpson, a greengrocer from Woolwich, started a freight transport business in 1902 and bought his first motor charabanc in 1912. The former South Eastern Metropolitan Tramways Company depot at Rushey Green, Catford, was purchased in 1920 for use as a head office, garage and coach station and in 1926 a limited company, A. Timpson & Sons Ltd, was formed. Services to many South and East coastal resorts were developed in the 1920s and by 1927 the company had become a major bus operator in the Hastings area. The Hastings operation was sold to Maidstone & District in 1933, leaving Timpson's to concentrate on its coastal express network. The company was jointly acquired by the BET group (60%) and Thomas Tilling Ltd (40%) in 1944 following the death of its founder. AECs had been popular since the 1920s and continued to be purchased regularly until the end of the company's existence. One of eight Reliances with Weymann Fanfare bodies taken into stock in 1958, VXP 507 is pictured at Victoria coach station in June 1964. *Geoff Lumb*

*Left:*
Timpson's acquired a number of operators over the years, the most notable being Bourne & Balmer of Croydon which had been established in 1920. It was taken over in 1953 and operated as a separate subsidiary for a few years. After it was wound up, certain Timpson's vehicles continued to carry Bourne & Balmer livery, including XXT 523, one of four Ford Thames Trader 570Es with Duple Yeoman bodies new in 1960. It is seen parked in Canterbury's Longport coach park in May 1964, alongside an AEC Reliance/Duple Britannia of the London Co-operative Society.
*David Warren*

*Left:*
Eight Reliances with Duple (Northern) Alpine Continental bodies arrived in 1963. The Alpine Continental was a development of the Continental which was designed and built at the former Burlingham factory in Blackpool and was Duple's first design for 36ft-long heavyweight coaches. 548 EYL was operating on hire to Midland Red when photographed at Llandudno in July 1968, by which time the traditional flag fleetname had been abandoned in favour of a simple lower case style.
*R. L. Wilson*

*Left:*
Harrington coachwork was also favoured during the period from 1959 to 1965. Two Wayfarer IVs arrived in 1959, followed by 10 Cavaliers in 1960 and 10 Grenadiers in 1964/5, all on AEC Reliance chassis. 555 GXX was one of the 1964 Grenadiers and is seen at Brighton in October of that year, parked next to a Bedford SB/Duple Bella Vega of Duval's, by then a subsidiary of the Royal Arsenal Co-operative Society. *David Warren*

*Left:*
Early in 1968 vehicles started to be repainted in a simplified version of the Bourne & Balmer grey and green livery. This became the standard scheme for a few years and is illustrated by CUW 561C, one of the 1965 batch of Reliance/Grenadiers, on a damp day in 1970 at Victoria coach station. This picture was taken in almost the same spot as the Reliance/Fanfare illustrated earlier, the background having changed completely by virtue of the office block, built in 1965, obscuring the BOAC terminal in Buckingham Palace Road. *Vic Nutton, courtesy Geoff Lumb collection*

*Left:*
Following the Harrington Grenadiers were two batches of Duple Commander bodied Reliances. JJJ 571D was one of the second batch, delivered in 1966. It had yet to succumb to the grey and green livery when photographed at Llandudno in July 1968. The 1966 Commanders introduced the simplified fleetname.
*R. L. Wilson*

*Left:*
Plaxton coachwork first appeared in the fleet in 1963, when four Reliances with Panorama bodies were delivered. Four more arrived in 1966, as illustrated by JJJ 573D, only two months old when seen at Southsea in April 1966. Plaxton then became the sole supplier of coachwork until 1973, when five Duple Dominant-bodied Reliances were purchased.
*David Warren*

*Right:*
A Bedford VAL demonstrator, 883 HMJ, was tried out for a few weeks in 1963, but it was not until 1968 that the company purchased any of the type. SJJ 587-90F carried Plaxton Panorama I bodies and were the first vehicles to be delivered in the grey and green livery. The first of the batch is illustrated here parked at Edward Street coach park, Brighton, in July 1968, sandwiched between a Bedford VAL/Duple Vega Major of Davis, Mitcham, and a Bristol LH/Plaxton Panorama of Golden Miller, Feltham.
*David Warren*

*Right:*
The livery was changed again in early 1972 to this white and purple scheme. This did not last long either, as Timpson's was absorbed into National Travel (South East) in January 1974 and consequently National white coach livery was adopted. Eight Reliances with Plaxton Panorama Elite II bodies arrived in 1972 and were the only vehicles to be delivered in white and purple. JYT 606-11K were 10m examples, while JYT 612/3K were 11m long. The last of the batch is seen turning from Millbank on to Lambeth Bridge in this October 1972 view. *Geoffrey Morant*

The United Services Transport Group was established in the late 1920s and was based in Balham, South London. A large fleet of coaches and lorries was built up and many routes to coastal resorts were developed, those to the east of London competing directly with the Ewer Group. In addition to the main United Services fleet, there were three subsidiary fleets: Blue Belle Coaching Services, L. Adnams and H. J. Phillips & Sons. United Services and Blue Belle shared a garage in Merton Road, Southfields, while Adnams' depot was in Merton High Street and Phillips had a garage at St John's Hill, Clapham Junction. Adnams was the only member of the group to retain its own livery, as shown here on 500 APJ, a 1956 Bedford SBO/Duple Vega. It was the last vehicle purchased by Adnams and was photographed in August 1964 at Cavendish Street, Brighton, parked alongside a similar vehicle of Mitcham Belle. *David Warren*

Six Bedford SB8s with Duple Bella Vega bodies entered the main United
Services fleet in 1963 and proved to be the last new vehicles for the group. The
coaching side of the business was sold to the Ewer Group in October 1965,
together with these six vehicles and four others. 852 FXP is depicted at
Brighton one year before the takeover, together with Blue Belle's OXT 309, a
1954 Bedford SBO with Duple Vega bodywork. *David Warren*

Messrs G. R. and W. D. Valli commenced business in 1927 trading as Valliant Coaches. A few years later, fellow local operator Falvey's of Ealing was taken over and became Falvey's Ealing Direct Coaches Ltd. The Valliant and Falvey's businesses were then combined to form Valliant Direct Coaches Ltd and in the ensuing years many other local operators were taken over allowing the company to expand. In addition to the usual AECs, Bedfords and Leylands, Valliant purchased a number of Beadle-Commer Rochester integral coaches during the 1950s. One of the first was 8 GMK which was entered when new in the 1956 Brighton Coach Rally. The blue coach on the right of the picture was another unusual vehicle, a Whitson-bodied Sentinel of Best & Sons, Wembley. *Geoffrey Morant*

*Below left:*
In 1965 Valliant Direct was taken over by Earls Court Holdings Ltd. The same holding company acquired Cronshaw's and its Venture Transport subsidiary in the following year and the three businesses were then merged to form Valliant-Cronshaw, based in Harrow. The newly combined company bought three 1964 AEC Reliances with Plaxton Panorama bodies from BTS of Coventry at the end of 1966, of which 448 CWK is seen in the following April at Edward Street, Brighton. *David Warren*

*Right:*
Five AEC Reliances and two Leyland Leopards, all with Duple Commander bodies, were added to the fleet in 1967. One of each type, URO 907E, a Reliance in standard livery and URO 902E, a Leopard in contract livery, pause at Basingstoke en route to Bournemouth in June 1971. Control of Valliant-Cronshaw passed to Hall's of Hounslow in 1969 and part of the business was sold again to a reactivated Venture Transport company in 1971. The Valliant name was used again by Kirby of Bushey in 1975 when it set up Valliant Coach Lines Ltd to take over the remains of Silverline Coaches, successors to Hall's of Hounslow. *Mike Barbour*

The original Venture Transport company was based at Hendon and was taken over by rival operator Cronshaw's in 1960. Heavyweight chassis types tended to be favoured, particularly Leylands. Tigers and Royal Tigers were followed in the 1950s by a number of Tiger Cubs, a chassis type more commonly used as a bus. 193 HMD, a 1956 example with a Duple Britannia body, was entered in the Brighton Coach Rally of that year and is parked on Madeira Drive between vehicles of two other London operators, a Bedford SB/Plaxton Venturer of Glenton Tours and an AEC Reliance/Weymann Fanfare of Timpson's. *Geoffrey Morant*

As mentioned previously, Venture Transport was re-established as a separate company in 1971, based in Harrow. Once again Leylands became the popular choice, although Bedfords were also purchased by the new company. DUR 965K was one of three Leopards with Plaxton Panorama Elite II bodies added to the fleet in 1972. In September of that year it had stopped for a refreshment break at the Devil's Punch Bowl, Hindhead, while en route to the coast with OJU 327F, an ex Valliant-Cronshaw Leopard with Duple Commander III bodywork. Control of Venture passed to Hearn's of Harrow Weald in 1985. *Cyril Cowland*

Mr Leslie Whyte, a civil servant, started operating a coach in his spare time to supplement his income. This was so successful that he gave up his Civil Service career to concentrate on his coach business. The company was based at Edgware and was registered as Whyte's (Edgware) Ltd. It specialised in the hire of executive coaches, but in 1964 airport contracts began to be operated. This side of the business expanded to such an extent that, in 1970, it was decided to dispose of the coach fleet and concentrate on airport work. The first executive coach to enter the fleet was LHM 999D, an AEC Reliance with Duple Commander bodywork. Named Whyte's Clipper, it had 36 reclining seats, a cocktail bar, a toilet and secretarial facilities. It was entered in the 1966 coach rallies at Blackpool and Brighton and scooped the Coach of the Year award at both events. It is about to receive its award at the Brighton event in this view. *David Warren*

*Left:*

Bloomfield Cars (London) Ltd of Camberwell had started operating coaches in the early 1960s, and in April 1964 it established a new company, World Wide Coaches Ltd, to develop the coach side of the business. World Wide specialised in high-class work, its most important customer being American Express Travel who had a shareholding in the company. A new depot in Coldharbour Lane, Camberwell, was opened in 1967. From 1964 a steady flow of AECs, Bedfords and Leylands entered the fleet, but in 1970 a Plaxton-bodied Mercedes-Benz 0302 was purchased. This unique vehicle, which had been exhibited at the Scottish Motor Show in November 1969, is pictured at Plough Lane, Wimbledon, in 1977. *Bob Wilkin*

*Left:*

A further 14 Mercedes-Benz 0302s were purchased in the following three years, but these were conventional integral vehicles. LGY 193K was one of nine delivered in 1972 and is seen in Hammersmith making its way along Hammersmith Road towards Kensington. The year 1972 saw the setting up of a new company, World Wide Coaches (Scotland) Ltd, to satisfy the need for a Scottish base. Ownership of the new company was shared equally between World Wide, American Express and Whiteford's of Lanark. In the same year the business of Phipps Blue Riband Tours of Bloomsbury was acquired. *Peter Tulloch collection*

The last AECs purchased were six 12m Reliances with Plaxton Panorama Elite III bodies. PGP 207L was pictured on Eccleston Bridge, Victoria, in April 1974, the month in which the Ewer Group gained control of the company by acquiring 70% of the shares, American Express continuing to hold the remaining 30%. In 1976 American Express sold their shareholding to the Ewer Group and World Wide thus became a wholly-owned subsidiary. Two years later, the Scottish branch was sold back to the Whiteford family. *Mike Barbour*

*Above:*
World Wide continued as a subsidiary of the Ewer Group until 1983. Standard Ewer Group vehicles were allocated to World Wide, as shown here by RYL 705R, a Bedford YMT/Duple Dominant II delivered in 1977. It is seen on Epsom Downs in the following June in company with Grey-Green MUL 689P, also a Bedford YMT but with the original style of Dominant body.
*Mike Barbour*

*Back cover:*
Valliant-Cronshaw was formed in 1966 following the purchase of the Lewis Cronshaw of Hendon and Valliant Direct of Ealing businesses by Earls Court Holdings. Six Leyland Leopard PSU3A/4Rs with Duple Commander III bodies were added to the fleet in 1968 and two of them, OJU 326F and OJU 328F, are pictured at Wembley Stadium in April 1970. *Alec Swain*